Therapy Cats, Dogs, and Rabbits

by Jenny Fretland VanVoorst

Consultant:
Bonnie V. Beaver
College of Veterinary Medicine
Texas A&M University

BEARPORT
PUBLISHING

New York, New York

Credits

Cover and Title Page, © Rob Goldman/Getty Images; 4, © Reporter/Shutterstock; 4–5, © Frances Roberts/Alamy; 6, © iStockphoto/Thinkstock; 6–7, © Dennis Sabo/Shutterstock; 8–9, © Golden Pixels LLC/Shutterstock; 10–11, © Karen Pulfer Focht, The Commercial Appeal/AP Images; 12–13, © Marmaduke St. John/Alamy; 14–15, © iofoto/Shutterstock; 16–17, © Juniors/SuperStock; 18, © Baronb/Shutterstock; 18–19, © Tyler Olson/Shutterstock; 20–21 © Sue McDonald/Shutterstock; 22T, © Golden Pixels LLC/Shutterstock; 22B, © iofoto/Shutterstock; 23T, © Dennis Sabo/Shutterstock; 23B, © iStockphoto/Thinkstock.

Publisher: Kenn Goin
Creative Director: Spencer Brinker
Photo Researcher: Arnold Ringstad
Design: Craig Hinton

Library of Congress Cataloging-in-Publication Data

Fretland VanVoorst, Jenny, 1972–
  Therapy cats, dogs, and rabbits / by Jenny Fretland VanVoorst.
    pages cm — (We work!: Animals with jobs)
  Audience: 7-12.
  Includes bibliographical references and index.
  ISBN-13: 978-1-61772-895-2 (library binding) — ISBN-10: 1-61772-895-0 (library binding)
  1. Domestic animals—Therapeutic use—Juvenile literature. 2. Pets—Therapeutic use—Juvenile literature. 3. Working animals—Juvenile literature. 4. Sick children—Care—Juvenile literature. I. Title.
  RM931.A65F74 2014
  615.8'5158—dc23

                                   2013008326

For more information, write to Bearport Publishing Company, Inc., 45 West 21st Street, Suite 3B, New York, New York 10010. Printed in the United States of America.

10 9 8 7 6 5 4 3 2 1

Contents

The Power of Pets 4

Furry Helpers 6

Pet Therapy Animals 8

Therapy Dogs in Hospitals 10

Therapy Dogs at School 12

Dogs and Cats in Nursing Homes.......14

Talking About Cats 16

Therapy Rabbits...................................18

A Helping Paw.....................................20

Glossary...22

Index 24

Read More 24

Learn More Online...............................24

About the Author................................24

The Power of Pets

Meet Peter.

He is a rabbit that helps people feel better.

How?

Peter is a **therapy animal**.

He visits people who are sick or feeling sad.

therapy animal

Petting and playing with Peter can cheer them up.

Peter the therapy rabbit

Furry Helpers

Therapy animals can be rabbits, cats, or dogs.

They all have an important job.

They visit people to make them feel better.

Some go to hospitals to comfort **patients**.

therapy kitten

Others work mainly in **nursing homes** to cheer up elderly people.

Some even help kids do better in school.

patient

Pet Therapy Animals

Pets need to pass a test to become therapy animals.

They must show that they are friendly with strangers.

They need to enjoy being petted and held, too.

Dogs must also be able to obey **commands** such as "sit" and "stay."

If a pet passes the test, it can become a therapy animal.

a dog obeying a "sit" command

9

Therapy Dogs in Hospitals

Some therapy dogs work in hospitals.

Their owners bring them to visit patients who are ill.

Petting and playing with the dogs helps people relax and heal faster.

an owner bringing his therapy dog to a hospital

Therapy Dogs at School

Some children have a hard time focusing on their schoolwork.

Bringing therapy dogs to classrooms can help these students.

Petting the dogs relaxes the students and reduces their stress.

This helps them stay calm and focused.

Dogs and Cats in Nursing Homes

People in nursing homes often do not have many visitors.

As a result, they can feel lonely.

Luckily, therapy animals are able to help out.

Cats can snuggle up in a person's lap and purr.

Dogs can give wet kisses.

Spending time with therapy animals helps people feel happier and less alone.

therapy dog owner

person in nursing home

15

Talking About Cats

Therapy cats can help young children who are having trouble speaking.

How?

The kids pet and play with the furry animals.

Then the kids are asked to talk about what they did.

therapy cat

16

Since the kids had so much fun, they are excited to speak.

Talking about the cats helps them become better speakers.

Therapy Rabbits

Like dogs, therapy rabbits visit patients in hospitals.

Unlike many dogs, however, they are small enough to sit in a person's lap.

As patients pet a rabbit's soft fur, they are able to relax.

When people are calm, they feel better.

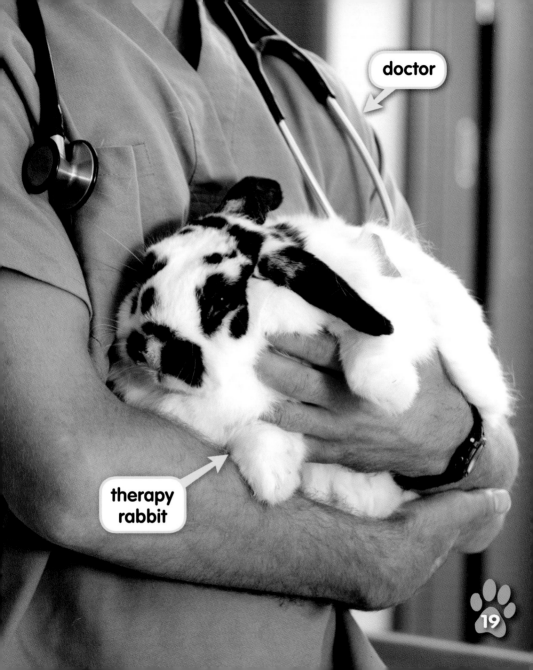

A Helping Paw

Therapy dogs, cats, and rabbits have important jobs to do.

They make sick people in hospitals feel better.

therapy dog in nursing home

They cheer up people in nursing homes.

They help children focus on their schoolwork and speak more easily.

Wherever they go, these animals are always ready to lend a helping paw!

Glossary

commands
(kuh-MANDS)
orders given by
someone to do
certain things

nursing homes
(NUR-sing HOHMZ)
places that care
for people who are
elderly or ill

patients
(PAY-shuhnts)
people who are
getting treatment
from a doctor

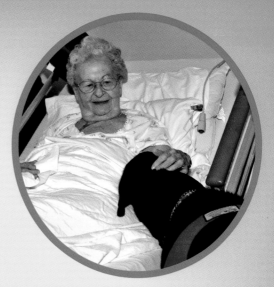

therapy animal
(THER-uh-pee
AN-uh-muhl)
an animal that visits
hospitals and other
places to cheer
people up and make
them feel better

23

Index

elderly people 7

hospitals 6, 10–11, 18, 20

nursing homes 7, 14–15, 20–21

school 7, 12

therapy cats 6, 14, 16–17, 20

therapy dogs 6, 8–9, 10–11, 12–13, 14, 18, 20

therapy rabbits 4–5, 6, 18–19, 20

training 8–9

Read More

Bozzo, Linda. *Therapy Dog Heroes (Amazing Working Dogs)*. Berkeley Heights, NJ: Bailey Books (2011).

Tagliaferro, Linda. *Therapy Dogs (Dog Heroes)*. New York: Bearport (2005).

Learn More Online

To learn more about therapy animals, visit
www.bearportpublishing.com/WeWork

About the Author

Jenny Fretland VanVoorst is a writer and editor of books for young people. She enjoys learning about all kinds of topics. When she is not reading and writing, Jenny enjoys kayaking, playing the piano, and watching wildlife. She lives in Minneapolis, Minnesota, with her husband, Brian, and their two pets.